ADVANCE PRAISE FOR
GRIEVING IS LOVING

"This book is filled with a deep wisdom that, when applied, can heal the pain and grief one experiences from losing a loved one."
—The Minimalists

"This inspiring book provides heartful reminders that love and grief are in an eternal embrace."
—Frank Ostaseski, author of *The Five Invitations: Discovering What Death Can Teach Us about Living Fully*

"This book is a gentle and kind guide to navigating the journey of loss and sorrow, keeping one company along the way."
—Narayan Helen Liebenson, author of *The Magnanimous Heart: Compassion and Love, Loss and Grief, Joy and Liberation*

"*Grieving Is Loving* is a good spiritual friend, a warm hand to anyone seeking companions in bearing the unbearable. With tender compassion and insight, Joanne Cacciatore walks with us shoulder to shoulder in our grief, bringing us into a world of tender vitality."
—Koshin Paley Ellison, author of *Wholehearted: Slow Down, Help Out, Wake Up* and an editor of *Awake at the Bedside: Contemplative Teachings on Palliative and End-of-Life Care*

"Even when every fiber of our being is quietly calling us to yield to the sacred shattering that is the grief experience, it can feel overwhelming to fully inhabit our pain and allow it to transform us. But we do not have to do it alone. Joanne Cacciatore's new book is a warm, loving, fiercely protective companion on the journey into the holy fire of loss. With this luminous collection of reflections from one of the foremost wisdom teachers on the alchemy of grief and loss, we can meet and bless the fullness of our experience as an offering of love to the one who has died and an affirmation of the innate wisdom of the broken-open heart."
—Mirabai Starr, author of *Caravan of No Despair* and *Wild Mercy*

"*Grieving Is Loving* is a wise, moving, and compassionate book. Reading it brought tears to my eyes as it reminded me of the loss of loved ones thirty and forty-five years ago. Not only should its message be read and internalized by those suffering the loss of a beloved, but also by those with friends who have lost or are likely to lose someone in the future—in other words, by everyone."
—Irving Kirsch, PhD, Harvard Medical School, University of Connecticut, University of Hull, author of *The Emperor's New Drugs: Exploding the Antidepressant Myth*

"The engaging sentiments in this book, shared by someone who has been there in the depths of grief, will provide comfort and confirmation to every bereaved person who opens it. This compilation of writing by some of the sharpest minds and sacred souls, including the author's, begs to be read, reread, and shared."
—Donna L. Schuurman, EdD, FT, senior director of advocacy and training, the Dougy Center for Grieving Children and Families

GRIEVING IS LOVING

Compassionate Words for Bearing the Unbearable

Joanne Cacciatore, PhD

Wisdom Publications
199 Elm Street
Somerville, MA 02144 USA
wisdomexperience.org

© 2020 by Joanne Cacciatore
All rights reserved.

No part of this book may be reproduced in any form or by any means,
electronic or mechanical, including photography, recording, or by any
information storage and retrieval system or technologies now known or
later developed, without permission in writing from the publisher.

Library of Congress Cataloging-in-Publication Data
Names: Cacciatore, Joanne, author.
Title: Grieving is loving: compassionate words for bearing the
unbearable / Joanne Cacciatore.
Description: Somerville, MA: Wisdom Publications, [2020] |
Includes index.
Identifiers: LCCN 2020024980 (print) | LCCN 2020024981 (ebook) |
ISBN 9781614297017 (paperback) | ISBN 9781614297024 (ebook)
Subjects: LCSH: Grief. | Love. | Consolation.
Classification: LCC BF575.G7 C275 2020 (print) |
LCC BF575.G7 (ebook) | DDC 155.9/37—dc23
LC record available at https://lccn.loc.gov/2020024980
LC ebook record available at https://lccn.loc.gov/2020024981

ISBN 978-1-61429-701-7   ebook ISBN 978-1-61429-702-4

24 23 22 21   5 4 3 2

Cover design by Jim Zaccaria. Interior design by Gopa & Ted2, Inc.

Printed on acid-free paper that meets the guidelines for permanence
and durability of the Production Guidelines for Book Longevity
of the Council on Library Resources.

Printed in United States of America.

Please visit fscus.org.

CONTENTS

Foreword by Johann Hari

IN THE UNITED States, many people have a startling experience when a loved one dies. Shortly after catastrophic loss—sometimes a day, or a week, or a month—they are told something jarring, often by a doctor. The distress they are feeling is often explained as abnormal, and all too often treated as a mental illness. Dr. Joanne Cacciatore's research has shown this is not a rare occurrence—with nearly one-half of grieving parents, for example, being prescribed psychiatric medication within a week after their painful loss.

For Dr. Jo, this is just one extreme manifestation of how we often respond to grief in our culture: as something shameful, abnormal, something to be shunted aside or suppressed. But for her, having done this work since 1996, grief is not a malfunction—grieving is not a sign that you have gone haywire and not an indication that something is broken and needs to be fixed. Rather, it is a sign you are a feeling—and loving—being. Grief is a form of love. This beautiful book will help you to see a more truthful, tender vision of what grief is—and how to live with it, rather than fight, manage, or avoid it.

To understand how Dr. Jo came to this vision, I think it might help you to picture her—as I do—in two different scenes, at two different moments in her life. She described the first to me when I interviewed her for my book *Lost Connections: Why You Are Depressed, and How to Find Hope*, and I'd like to recount some of that now.

Many years ago, in 1994, her doctor reassured her when, at the end of a long pregnancy, she expressed concern about her baby's well-being. "Oh honey," he said, "you just need some attention." She had been having extremely painful contractions for three weeks, and she thought the baby needed help. She was a very diligent mother-to-be—she wouldn't even chew gum with aspartame in it because she was worried it might harm her baby. So she kept insisting: "These are really painful contractions—they don't feel normal to me." But the doctor repeatedly placated her: "It's normal."

When she finally went into labor, she sensed quite quickly that there was something wrong. There was chaos all around her, and the medical team was visibly panicked. She would have a contraction that lasted for a minute, then thirty seconds later, she'd have another contraction. She says that the birth was so traumatic that she "left her body" and couldn't stop quivering.

As soon as her eight-pound daughter, Cheyenne,

emerged, they handed her to her father, and he said gently, "We have a beautiful little girl." At that moment, "I just sat up," she told me years later. "I reached my hands out—I said, 'give her to me.' She was perfect. She had rolls of fat under her cheeks. Her little wrists had little rolls of fat. And he put her in my arms. She looked peacefully asleep and my brain could not wrap around that she was dead. It was a strange juxtaposition of birth and death that coalesced in a single moment—and that would change the course of my life."

"Now I will tell you," she said to me, "I've had a lot of loss in my life. I'd lost both my parents and my best friend in my thirties." But she could never have prepared to lose one of her children. It's was an unbearable, unfathomable loss. Three months after her daughter died, she weighed barely ninety pounds. "I wasn't sure I was going to make it," she said. "It felt like I was dying. Every day, I would open my eyes—if I slept—and say: I don't want to be here. I don't want to be here. I don't want to feel like this any more. I can't do this anymore."

She was catapulted into a new identity, a grieving mother, and she would have to find a way to integrate grief into a life she had never wanted, never planned, and feared terribly.

The second scene in which I would like you to picture Dr. Jo is today, at the Selah Carefarm, a community of grievers she built with the MISS Foundation where beauty and pain, love, and grief intersect. Every month, those who have experienced trauma and grief come to talk about their grief and to work with any of Dr. Jo's forty rescue animals. This is a model of those who have suffered helping those who have suffered, those in pain helping others in pain. One of my oldest and closest friends lost her five-year-old son to a brain tumor, and she is one of the many mothers who has fallen into compassionate arms—and hooves—there at Selah Carefarm. Dr. Jo helped her to see that she doesn't have to fight her grief.

Dr. Jo responded to her own loss by opening a space inside her own heart where she can be open to the pain of others—and she helped my friend to do the same. When she came back to Britain, my friend told me it was the first time, since her son's passing, that she felt truly understood, and like her pain made sense.

Following Cheyenne's death, Dr. Jo went back for her PhD, and she is now a professor of social work at Arizona State University. She came to think that the pathologizing of grief in American culture is a deep error, one that worsens people's pain, exacerbates their loneliness and confusion, and compromises their self-trust. "To me, it's the greatest insult," she told me "It's not just an insult to grief and to the relationship with the person who has died, but it's an insult to love. I mean—why do we grieve? If my neighbor across the street died, and I don't know my neighbor, I might say, 'Oh, that's so sad for his family'—but I don't grieve. But when I love the person, I grieve. We grieve because we have loved." To say grief is pathological or abnormal when it lasts beyond an artificially determined time limit, or to imply that it is a disease to be treated with drugs, is to deny the core of our very being-ness. Even animals mourn their dead, she shared, as did J35—an orca whale nicknamed "Tahlequah," who was observed by scientists to have carried the body of her dead baby, with the help of her pod, for seventeen days through the Pacific Ocean.

Far from being irrational, Dr. Jo says, the pain of grief is necessary. "I don't even want to recover from her death," she says about her daughter, Cheyenne. "Staying connected to the grief helps me to do my work with such a full, compassionate heart," and to live as fully as she can.

And, she adds, being connected to her grief helped her understand the pain of others in a way she couldn't before. "It makes me stronger," she says, "even in my vulnerable places."

Grieving Is Loving is a book of profound compassion and wisdom and strength—and it's the best kind of strength: the kind that comes not from fighting and suppressing pain, but from going to our most vulnerable places in a spirit of deep love. As you're about to see, Dr. Jo is teaching us how to grieve, and in doing so, she is teaching us how to love—how to love the people we have lost, and to love our own wounds, and what they can now inspire us to do to honor those who are gone.

Johann Hari is the author of *Lost Connections: Uncovering the Real Causes of Depression—and the Unexpected Solutions* and has written for publications including *The Independent* and *The Huffington Post*. He has also given TED talks on the topics of addiction, depression, and anxiety.

PREFACE

W HEN I PUBLISHED *Bearing the Unbearable*, my first book with Wisdom Publications in 2017, I was surprised and overwhelmed by the response. I continue to receive hundreds of emails a month from grieving people around the world, from South Africa to Norway, about how the book made them feel like they had a friend who spoke the same language. Many told me they'd read it in just one or two sittings because it was "unputdownable."

Bereaved mom of Logan said that because her "pain is with (her) every day and it never stops," people often move away from her grief rather than toward her grief—and that means that people move away from *her* too. She continued to share that while reading *Bearing the Unbearable*, she felt validated: "I don't feel alone, and I don't feel crazy. I wish I could make everyone I know read it." Another woman, Deb, whose spouse died tragically, said, "Your book has spoken to me more than any of the therapy, coaching, spiritual seeking, soul seeking that I have done since his death."

This book, meant to be a companion in grief to people

like this (and like you), contains some select thoughts from *Bearing the Unbearable*—and so much more. This new book is for anyone who has lost another who is so beloved that their heart feels shattered beyond repair. When you feel the pull of your grief, when sadness or anger or despair ask to be seen, take this book to a quiet corner, outside in the sun or in your room or where you feel respite, and read from wherever in the book you are called to read.

I hope this book will be a companion for you through your grief, a sanctuary for your broken heart. I hope it offers a meditative place to turn toward your broken heart in moments of feeling deeply. I hope it will be a salve—not for grief but for the loneliness that often accompanies it. May this book become a comrade in your journey through loss.

This book was written in the midst of immense global suffering during the 2020 pandemic. There have been many deaths, much loss, and collective dread such as I've never seen in my lifetime. Many are more afraid, lonely, confused, and frustrated than they've ever been. All these overwhelming emotions are, at least in part, what many grieving people face every day. Those of us grieving the death of a much-loved person are acutely aware of mortality and the vulnerability of others we love. We put our feet on the floor and bravely face our own dramatically changed worlds. We confront loneliness when others turn away from our grief, forget to call or text, don't say the names of our children and siblings and parents and spouses.

When such events happen, be they collective or individual, nothing is the same, ever again. We have been awakened by the catastrophic loss of someone we deeply love.

And when we are awake, when we have already known deep loss, we know this risk exists every moment of every day. Babies die. Toddlers die. Children die. Teenagers die. Young adults die. Middle-aged adults die. Older adults die. Animals die. All living things die.

But right now, more than perhaps ever in history, the world has paused to recognize this reality. Usually, the world pays no attention to death until it's personal. But now, the world, as a collective whole, is suffering even if not actually mourning.

I've been telling others, the not-yet-grievers, to remember the suffering of the world right now because this will help us all be more understanding, more compassionate, and more authentic with those who are grieving the death of someone they love, now and in the future, both within and outside the effects of the pandemic.

Let this transform us all; let it move us all toward compassion.

Let's not go back to life as usual.

Because for many, when someone we love deeply dies,

life is not "normal"—not yesterday, not today, and not tomorrow. Life is forever changed.

We feel grief because we have deeply loved. And while this hurts, most of us would not return one moment with that person, even if it meant the promise of abated grief.

Our beloved dead are worth our pain. They are worth our tears. They are worth remembering.

May we all live in compassion,
Dr. Jo

INTRODUCTION: HONEST GRIEF

I F YOU HAVE lost someone to death, the person you miss most in the world, part of your essential existence, I am so sorry.

I am not "so sorry" in the politely cliché or automatonic way: I am so sorry in an unspeakable and "there really aren't words for this" way. I feel great sorrow for you and with you.

In the beginning after catastrophic loss, many will show up in ways that feel hopeful. They will send flowers and cards, meals and hugs. We may not remember much about this part. Our systems have endured a tremendous shock. Nothing inside us wants to stay where it is: not our hearts or our minds or our bodies. It's too painful, too terrifying to live in a world where something so very precious can die. We may get glimpses of the hospital, funeral, or food train, but those memories may feel unreal, intangible, and so—understandably—the thank-you cards collect dust on our desks.

Days and weeks and months may pass where large swathes of time are unrecollectable. Our entire existence has shifted. Even the image in the mirror is unfamiliar. Our own sensory experiences of the world change—sound, taste, touch, sight, proprioception feel altered—time has a completely different and irrelevant quality. We may feel as if we're living in a liminal space between the living and the dead, an alternate reality from which there is no escape. And yet in quiet moments when we notice our own irregular breathing and contemplate all we've irretrievably lost, it's simply too much grief to bear and too little mercy to spare for our shattered-open hearts.

Mostly, there is this fog of disbelief that lingers as we move in and out of consciousness, wondering if this is a nightmare from which we can awaken.

Day by day—sometimes minute by minute—the grief will strike and bring us to our knees. It will surprise us in grocery stores and libraries, at work and at public events. Our minds may begin to tell stories that might or might not belong to us: stories about our goodness as a parent or person or about what we could've or should've or would've done differently. We may feel the relentless sting of shame, guilt, and regret. Our minds may start to question whether we loved our child enough, or it may ask if he or she knew that love. Some days we will feel frenetic, desperately discursive and ungrounded. Other days we may resign ourselves to the lethargy and complacence of this unsolvable tragedy.

Our bodies hurt. Our brains stop working. Our hearts feel heavy, laden with the weight of loss. Few things, if any, matter anymore, not the mortgage or the rotting leftovers or the pool algae or the missed calls and texts. Every relationship in our lives changes, for better or not, and every relationship to inanimate objects and the universe and animals and trees and our past and future will change too. This unsteadiness will puzzle others.

And a visually specific "what the hell happened?" film will loop through our minds, its irremediable ending is the unsatisfactory same, over and over, until it feels like we've descended into madness. Yet every bit of this enactment—all this emotional rising and falling—is normal. The only wrongness, the only madness or pathology, is that our beloved died.

Months will pass, and ever so slowly our memories may begin to re-emerge with shreds of trauma and terror and disappointment and hopelessness. The imperfectly beautiful life that was once ours doesn't exist in the same way, and we try to find steady ground from which to be reborn.

Just around this time, when the permanence of our loved one's absence begins sinking into our marrow, other people, because they've been taught this myth, will think it's time for us to move on—to get over it—to reconcile the irreconcilable. At the core, these directives don't make sense because they are nonsensical. The intimation that our child's death is akin to the loss of something replaceable, something to be healed with iodine and a Band-Aid or a prayer and prescription, feels even more isolating. Our hearts, then, may begin to question their own wisdom: "Should I move on?" "What does 'moving on' even mean?" "Am I grieving too much? Too little? Too openly? Too privately? Am I crazy?"

But others don't know, even when they are well-meaning. They cannot know this bottomless grief. Still, their expectations may cause us to mistrust our own wise hearts, our own authentic emotions. And because everything in our world has drastically changed and has been unapologetically stolen from us, there is now no poverty of doubt, fear, and suffering. Only now, it feels even more solitary.

Because of this, some will abandon us. In the aisle between the Cheerios and applesauce, they turn and run. Some will try, clumsily perhaps, to abbreviate our grief with their platitudes: "All things happen for a reason," "At least he's not in pain," "God has a plan," "She'd want you to just be happy," "Just let go," and "Time heals all wounds."

And some, thankfully, will show up with their unassuming hearts open and climb with us into the abyss. Those are the best kind, and we will soon learn who is safe and who is reckless with our fragile hearts.

And this is where it gets tricky, because the mind sometimes internalizes toxic cultural fiction about grief that is dangerous.

Messages from within a culture that avoids and pathologizes grief—within medicine, religion, education, and social life—will urge us to question ourselves and our righteous emotional experiences after loss. Some of those messages will even confront and challenge our desire to remain connected to our beloved dead. Abandoning grief, they say, is necessary for the promise of being happy again.

These same sideline speculators will assert that grief is to be loathed and avoided because it comes with ugly machinations that scare us and others. Understandably, there is a draw to resist the spiral into this darkest night of the soul, and the resistance comes with—often unconscious—distractions. Distracting temptations to avoid our grief are cleverly disguised and endless: work, food, television, gambling, drugs, alcohol—anything that takes us away from our grief feels like relief.

No doubt these may be a welcome respite from the pain, even if only momentarily. But these short-lived and superficial attempts to palliate grief simply prolong the inevitable. Grief will come, one way or another, even if it is forced to change and hide its real form.

The tempter's promise is a trap that will fragment and chronically constrict our entire world. The only way to stop feeling grief is to stop feeling.

Right in the center of our very wise hearts is the realization that we feel extraordinary grief because of extraordinary love. If we can become still enough, if we can listen to our hearts, they know that grief is not the enemy. The sagacious heart knows that grief is just an innocent outcome of a most unnatural loss. What we really hate, the real enemy, is that our beloved died. That is what we wish we could conquer, undo, overcome, beat, negotiate, and avoid. Grief is a clean and honest product of the worse day of our lives.

Even as years pass, some will say that it's unhealthy to remember. Some will castigate us for regrieving. Some will say to choose happiness instead of grief. But happiness and grief are not competitors. That is a myth perpetrated by a culture that is foolishly obsessed with pursuing one and dangerously avoiding the other.

Yes, years later, decades later, we will still carry with us this consummate grief. We will carry it as long as we are alive and willing to live honestly and fully. As the tidal waves of grief come and go, we become more adept at navigating them.

So the invitation for us—from the genesis of loss—will be to mourn openly with our fists raised high, standing strong against those who would try to, again, take what is rightfully ours.

Haven't we already lost enough? Need we lose our truth, too?

This is the one thing we can control; we do have our own power here.

With the compassionate support of safe people, when

we are ready, we can rise up, holding our grief in one fist and our love in the other: "This is mine, and you have no right to take it!"

We can reclaim our power in grief, reclaim what is ours. And we can fight to keep safe what has been and will always be the most holy parts of us: our beloved ones who died and for whom we will grieve as long as we are separated.

And we should all know there will likely be peripheral losses along the way.

Many of us will have to make hard decisions. We may be stuck in a meaningless job. Losing our beloved one certainly augments our perspective. Our faith communities may not meet our needs, and we may choose to worship elsewhere. And relationships may crack under the stress of death's fallout. The question: "Is this relationship worth saving?" may be one we often visit.

Because when we are living grief honestly, some people will fall away, like leaves from a mighty oak in a winter storm. They are not ready. Perhaps they don't have the capaciousness for this reluctant and painful transformation.

Let them fall softly.

Shed the judging stories that are not our own and that do not serve us.

We can immerse ourselves, instead, in the sacred grief shared by others across space and through history who know and who, too, raise their fists and stand tall in their truth.

It may take time to find our tribe, but when we do, there will be mutual recognition and wordless knowing in the others' eyes. Few things are as simultaneously comforting and painful as this meeting.

We can learn when to rest our weary bodies and put down the weight of grief for a while, always returning to it, or let someone else help us carry it until we're strong enough for solo carrying. We can turn toward it when it asks to be seen. It will call us, and if we don't answer for a very long time, it will come in the side door and bring other, even undesirable, guests who aren't connected to our truth.

We can reach deep into the center of our core and summon the courage to live in this truth: our grief is part of us now.

This truth will make our lives bigger not smaller.

We can practice fully inhabited grief, letting it move cellularly through our being. It will transform us for sure. Remember that we are already being reluctantly transformed, no matter how much we resist. Things will change; it's a matter of direction and tenor now. Grief, especially when traumatic, can shut us down and disconnect us, or it can shatter our hearts into a million pieces of fierce compassion in the world. One way or another, we change.

We can remind ourselves that even on days when it

doesn't feel like it, there is strength in weakness, and there is power in surrender.

The energy of grief is a more powerfully vital force than the destructive energy of avoidance. And that force will, one day, be the very force that saves our own lives and maybe the very worthy lives of many others.

And no matter what, no one and nothing can take from us what is ours, once we trust it.

We will not cease to exist if we grieve our truth.

We will cease to exist if we don't.

GRIEVING IS LOVING

Grief comes to one and all; no one is exempt.
We must remember our dead.
We must do better for the bereaved.
We must embody compassion.
To be redeemed we must remember.
Remembering is our duty—
and the only thing that will save us.

• • •

Life is tragic simply because the earth turns and the sun inexorably rises and sets, and one day, for each of us, the sun will go down for the last, last time—
—JAMES BALDWIN

• • •

When a person beloved by us dies, our lives can become unbearable. And yet we are asked—by life, by death—to bear it, to suffer the insufferable, to endure the unendurable. "Bearing the Unbearable" is an expression of my own heart and my life's work—demanding and formidable, satisfying and deeply vital.

{ 13 }

To fully inhabit grief is to hold the contradictions of the great mystery that loss shatters us and we become whole. Grief empties us and we are filled with emotion. Fear paralyzes us and we lend courage to another. We mourn our beloveds' absence and we invoke their presence. We cease to exist as we once were and we become more fully human. We know the darkest of all nights and in so doing can bring the light of our loved ones into the world. We are the paradox. We are the bearers of the unbearable.

• • •

I would rather live in a world where my life is surrounded by mystery than live in a world so small that my mind could comprehend it.
—HARRY EMERSON FOSDICK

• • •

We mourn for tomorrow's moments, and next month's moments, and next year's moments; we mourn at the graduations and weddings, the births, and the deaths that follow. Grief consists of countless particles, countless moments, each one of which can be mourned. And through them all, we always know in our very cells that someone is missing, that there is a place in our hearts that can never be filled.

Grief and love occur in tandem.

Death feels savage, and to some extent, it is—but grief need not be vilified. Over time, grief can morph from a dreaded, unwanted intruder to something more familiar and less terrifying—a companion, perhaps.

For all who love, suffering is inevitable.

Make no mistake: losing someone we love deeply changes us, inescapably and for all time, and it is painful beyond all imagining. It is through inhabiting, often painfully, our emotions that we are able to become fully human. Through grief, we can experience an alchemical transformation that cannot be contrived, hastened, or imparted by others.

Once upon a time, the world was right.
And when the world was right,
our hearts beat together.

The future included us.
Together.
And when the world was right,
I could speak your name without pangs,
and all my plans centered on our togetherness.

And when my well-planned world contained you,
it was a beautiful life.

I never planned for this apartness.
I never planned for the collapsing grief of your absence.
I never imagined, and still cannot,
that this could be my life.

I just miss my right world.
I just miss you.

> **And we wept that one so lovely should have a life so brief.**
> —WILLIAM CULLEN BRYANT

When others call into question our grief, defy our perennial relationship with those we love who have died, treat us as anathema and avoid us, and push us toward healing before we are ready, they simply redouble our burden.

• • •

It almost seems that the only way to eradicate our grief would be to relinquish the love we feel—to disassemble our loved one's place in our lives. But checking in with the wisdom of our hearts, we see that is impossible.

> **May there be such a oneness between us that when one weeps the other tastes salt.**
> —KAHLIL GIBRAN

To love means to open ourselves to grief, sorrow, and disappointment as well as to joy, fulfillment, and thus an intensity of consciousness that before we did not know was possible.

—ROLLO MAY

• • •

When we are frightened and in pain, we need others with whom we can be honest. We need others who can enter the abyss with us, sometimes again and again. We need to reach out to someone who is safe, who will not judge, who will not shut down or shun our pain. And, when we are hurting this much, we may need to borrow, muster, or scrape up the courage to *reach out* to others. And we need these things for an indefinite period. Because there are some losses from which there exists no end to grief.

Choices we make as grievers merit the deference of others.

Solace and care come from many sources. Others who listen deeply, attentively, and nonjudgmentally can be found in the least expected places. Take note, pay attention, and seek help from those willing to be present with you.

Time with these kinds of people can carry you through perilous terrain.

Grief, with no fixed expiration date, is an inescapable truth of the human condition. Grief, by its very nature, is labyrinthine and enigmatic; its implications are emotional, physical, social and interpersonal, economic, spiritual, and existential.

• • •

Every year I manage to live on this earth I collect more questions than answers.
—FATIMAH ASGHAR

• • •

RECIPE FOR RAW GRIEF

FROM THE KITCHEN OF THERESA'S HEART

SERVES: ONE

ingredients:

1 heaping cup disbelief

1 tablespoon reluctance
to say good-bye

16 ounces excruciating pain

3 cups brutal sadness

2 tablespoons confusion
(substitute questioning)

½ cup constant obsessing

8 ounces anger (substitute
feeling misunderstood)

2 teaspoons agonizing guilt

¾ cup embarrassment

1 quart loneliness

Dash of untimely and
needless

DIRECTIONS: Preheat oven to 1,123°F. In small bowl, mix disbelief with reluctance to say good-bye. Next, trim platitudes from excruciating pain and discard. Use mixture to coat pain. Cook in scalding cast-iron skillet until blackened. Set aside. Fill large pot with tears and bring to a boil. Lower heat; pour brutal sadness into pot and cover. Allow to simmer for weeks. When sadness is numb, remove from heat and drain tears from pot. Stir confusion and constant obsessing into sadness and set aside. Use mallet to pound anger until tender. Cut into bite-size pieces. Fry in pan over high heat with agonizing guilt and embarrassment. When anger turns red, remove pan from heat. To assemble, spread pain into bottom of baking dish. Layer on the sadness mixture, then cover with anger, guilt, and shame.

Top with loneliness. Season with untimely and needless. Place in oven and bake until loneliness turns to intense longing. Let sit for a lifetime.

NOTES: *Pairs well with absolute fear. Best served smothered in love and compassion (may need assistance). Garnish with a sense of peace.*

• • •

The depth and breadth of the loss is unfathomable, and its full impact is never realized immediately, but only gradually over time. The mind tries to protect us from near-lethal initial shock, and a type of emotional anesthesia often ensues so that we may feel as if we are in a movie or operating in slow motion. Sounds, figures, and movements change, and we may exist in a profoundly altered state of consciousness.

• • •

Grief education is quintessential to shifting our culture's antagonistic relationship to grief, and expressive, creative arts are an important part of this.

> **Until my ghastly tale is told,
> this heart within me burns.**
> —SAMUEL TAYLOR COLERIDGE

Slowly, as the shock of loss gradually withdraws its numbing veil, an indescribable pain arises from the innermost pit of our bellies. This pain brings with it feelings we may never have felt—unfamiliar and hideously distressing. Everything in us wants to run from the reality of loss, yet the agony demands to be felt. It calls and recalls our attention repeatedly to the details. In a sense, the process of mourning is an outward expression of that love that now has no physical or interpersonal place to be enacted.

. . .

It's not unusual for bereaved parents, children, siblings, grandparents, and spouses to experience damage to their sense of self, persistent yearning for the one who died, and a desire to escape the pain by any means—including death of the self. Many parents with whom I've worked tell me they feel their old selves, the people they were, have died. Some people report feelings of guilt and shame at their loved one's death—even when, from the outside, these emotions seem unjustified. These feelings are common and normal, albeit painful, for those grieving a significant loss. Deep despair, agitation and impatience, apathy, anhedonia, and a lack of interest in things that once mattered are also frequently reported—and also quite normal.

When grief asks to be seen, meet it and embrace it as you would a visit from an old friend.

What parent whose child has died would not experience a yearning to reestablish that potent bond? What child would not feel unsafe, afraid, and abandoned in the world when his or her parent dies? What person would not experience a sometimes crushing loneliness upon the death of a partner? What brother or sister would not intensely long for another hug from the other person who shared a childhood?

...

When our beloved dies, we become acutely aware of death, our own and others' finitude, in a phenomenon termed *mortality salience*, and we begin to grapple with this reality.

Envy toward others who still have what we have lost often arises, and anger—even rage—may also come up.

• • •

There is, I am convinced, no picture that conveys in all its dreadfulness, a vision of sorrow, despairing, remediless, supreme. If I could paint such a picture, the canvas would show only a woman looking down at her empty arms.

—CHARLOTTE BRONTË

• • •

In a grieving family, suffering happens at the individual and collective levels. Every person is grieving and acting out that grief in his or her own way, and each person is enacting that grief in relationship to others.

• • •

Many grievers feel implicit or explicit social pressure to "feel better" or "move on," and the incongruence between the messages of how they should feel and the inner wisdom of what they actually *do* feel causes many to doubt their own hearts. This lack of alignment between self and the other is one more way in which *avoidable* and *irrational* suffering is imposed on grievers in the middle of *natural*— which is to say unavoidable and rational—suffering.

**There is no greater agony than bearing
an untold story inside you.**

—DR. MAYA ANGELOU

To help those grieving, society needs to provide us all a place to rest our minds and hearts: a place fertile with loving kindness and compassion—not judgment, coercion, and scrutiny. Only there, only when ready, will we be able to blossom (albeit painfully) into a joy that cohabitates with grief—rather than displacing or replacing it.

• • •

Others may tell us that it's time to "move on" or that this is "part of some bigger plan"—because our shattering makes them feel uneasy, vulnerable, at risk. Some may avoid us, others pity us. But this grief is ours. We have earned this grief, paying for it with love and steadfast devotion. We own this pain, even on days when we wish it weren't so. We needn't give it away or allow anything, or anyone, to pilfer it. Through the grief and the love we can hold our heads high—even in tears, even shattered. What's ours is ours—and *rightfully*.

> **Though I think not to think about it,**
> **I do think about it and shed tears**
> **thinking about it.**
>
> —RYOKAN

The circumstances surrounding deaths that are traumatic in nature may be severely worsened by the way people are notified of death; by unskillful grief-denying therapy; and by legalities and insensitive actions—medical, spiritual, and community-based—that do not take into account the context of trauma and its effects.

· · ·

This is my path. It was not a path of my choice, but it is a path I must walk mindfully and with intention. It is a journey through grief that takes time. Every cell in my body aches. I may be impatient, distracted, frustrated, and unfocused. I won't want to celebrate anything. I may get angry more easily, or I may seem hopeless. I will shed many, many, many tears. I won't smile as often as my old self did. Smiling hurts now. Most everything hurts some days, even breathing.

But please, just sit beside me.
Say nothing.

Do not offer a cure.
Or a pill, or a word, or a potion.
Witness my suffering and don't turn away from me. Please be gentle with me.

Please, self, be gentle with me, too.

I will not ever "get over it," so please don't urge me down that path. Even if it seems like I am having a good day, maybe I am even able to smile for a moment, the pain is just beneath the surface of my skin. My chest has a nearly constant sinking pain, and sometimes I feel as if I will explode from the grief.

Don't tell me how I should or shouldn't be doing it or that I should or shouldn't "feel better by now." Don't tell me that "God has a plan" for me. Don't tell me what's right or wrong. I'm doing it my way, in my time.

I have a new normal now. Oh, perhaps as time passes, I will discover new meanings and insights about what her death means to me. Perhaps, one day, when I am very old, I will say that time has truly helped to heal my broken heart. But always remember that not a second of any minute of any hour of any day passes when I am not aware of the presence of her absence, no matter how many years lurk over my shoulder.

Please, be kind to me. 🌿

When someone we love dies traumatically, we feel frighteningly uprooted, markedly insecure, and our ability to trust in the world feels gravely threatened—and indeed it *is* gravely threatened.

Practice being with grief unconditionally and nonjudgmentally.

Society pushes mourners to assign more negative self-judgments and erroneous meaning to their grief reactions. This may include ascribing to ourselves inadequate adjustment ("I should feel better by now."); personal incompetence ("What is wrong with me?"); or even mental illness ("I have major depression."). Such erroneous beliefs about grieving lead to suppression, distraction, and avoidance of natural grief reactions—in short, they lead to vastly more suffering.

🌿 The Story of the Missing Jigsaw Puzzle Piece

We finished the puzzle—except for one last piece. The missing piece belonged in the upper right, near the corner—a small fragment of azure sky.

"I don't have it," he said.
"It must be here somewhere," I told him.
We looked around, under the couch and table, in the closet, standing up and spinning, but we could not find that missing piece. I even offered the kids a reward, one dollar, if they found it. Even so, they quickly lost interest—as children do—and retreated to their sunroom.

And then it hit me.
Of course there was a missing piece.
Looking at the almost-completed puzzle, I could see the vast beauty of the scene—but there was a piece missing. And every time I looked at that puzzle, before I would be able to appreciate the beauty in the picture, I would first see that there, right there, is a hole—a missing piece.

And nothing but that one specific, unique piece could ever fit in that spot. 🌿

We have only one reality and that is the here and now. What we miss by our evasions will never return. . . . Each day is precious: a moment can be everything.

—KARL JASPERS

• • •

How do we bear that which is unbearable? How do we suffer that which is insufferable? How do we endure that which is unendurable? Early grief feels wild, primitive, nonlinear, and crazed. It commands our assent and our attention; it uses up all the oxygen in the room; it erupts unpredictably. Our minds replay grief-related content in habitual cycles. It feels inescapable and lasts for much longer than other people, the nonbereaved, think it should. Like an open, bleeding wound, it begs our tending. "I am here," grief says. "Be careful with me. Stop. Pause. Stay with me."

When we learn to *be with* grief, to surrender to it—we then find we can do something with it.

Contemplating the death of those we love and feeling tremendous grief in the aftermath brings us face-to-face with what matters. It shows us what it means to be human is to be vulnerable, to suffer, and to risk love.

• • •

Love anything, and your heart will certainly be wrung and possibly be broken.... The only place outside Heaven where you can be perfectly safe from all the dangers and perturbations of love is Hell.
—C.S. LEWIS

• • •

The pause is an art—and as such it is much like grieving. The pause is what happens between words, between breaths, and between moments of what is and what isn't. We remember to hold and take a few deep, slow, long breaths.

The road up and the road down is one and the same.
—HERACLITUS

To love deeply is one of life's most profound gifts, and the loss of a loved one is one of life's most profound tragedies.

• • •

There is an enormous hidden cost for us, as humans, to our culture's relentless obsession with happiness: we lose our willingness and ability to be vulnerable, and we forfeit our connection to self, other, and the natural world—and most especially to our honest, authentic, legitimate grief.

• • •

For some, it may seem strange to speak of feeling grief and gratitude simultaneously. For others, if we can set aside the pursuit-of-happiness zeitgeist, this is unadulterated truth.

Beauty and pain coexist.

Being happy does not mean we do not feel pain or grief or sadness—successively or, often, simultaneously. Sorrow and contentment, grief and beauty, longing and surrender coexist in the realm of sameness. This is called the unity of opposites, and it liberates us from a myopic, dualistic view of our emotions as *either/or*. We are not either happy or sad. We are not either grieving or grateful. We are not either content or despairing. We are *both/and*.

———————————

We practice accepting whatever we feel, moment by moment, without trying to change it. In this way we gradually come to experience a peace with what *truly* is.

———————————

Even in moments of joy or lightness, we still know grief—because there is always this ongoing longing for our loved one, for their voice, for their hug, for their touch, for their simple presence. We may also feel grateful for what we have even as we experience despair over what we've lost.

• • •

Any joy I experience throughout life is not contingent on things going my way, on having no losses, no disappointments, and no (more) deaths. Most important, it's not dependent on forbidding grief to come and go as I know it will for the entire duration of my own life.

The danger of trying to bypass grief is that grief then comes out sideways, only now unrecognizable as a legitimate product of loss. In the words of the existential psychotherapist Irvin Yalom, "The pain is there; when we close one door on it, it knocks to come in somewhere else." Or as the poet Rumi puts it, "Some torn places cannot be patched."

Because you love, you will experience grief.

Grief—especially traumatic grief—asks to be seen, and it will wait until we see it, though if grief is asked to wait too long, it may change form, sometimes becoming toxic and poisoning our very souls.

...

Seeking only the "good" emotions and avoiding the "bad" emotions is problematic even for those not suffering the death of a loved one. Cutting ourselves off from any genuine feeling in order to pursue or manufacture another feeling denies our truth. When we reclaim what belongs to us—the pain of our grief, for instance—then we need no longer feel acrimony toward it, and we need no longer expend our valuable energy trying to be rid of that which we wish were not ours. We can simply—or complicatedly—*let it be*.

• • •

Whatever comes, we let it be as it is. When we do this, we come to see, in this moment or the next, our emotions always moving. The word *emotion* has its roots in the Latin *movere* and *emovere* meaning "to move through" and "to move out." Our emotions move in us, move through us, and move between us. And when we allow them to move freely, they change, perhaps scarcely and perhaps gradually—but inevitably. This is grief's most piercing message: *there is no way around—the only way is through*.

• • •

You think your pain and your heartbreak are unprecedented in the history of the world, but then you read. It was books that taught me that the things that tormented me most were the very things that connected me with all the people who were alive, or who had ever been alive.

—JAMES BALDWIN

**Like love, grief can't be constrained
by time and space.**

To bypass grief, we must also bypass love. We, as modern humans, are experts in bypassing grief and trauma, cutting ourselves off from pain. Fear drives bypass—curtailing authentic feelings—and bypass leaves us psychologically imprisoned by our own fear. Then we become too frightened to allow our love to flow out, and we build high walls around our hearts to self-protect. In so doing, though, we cut ourselves off from humanity—our own and everyone else's.

**Spirituality is a way *into* suffering,
not the way out of it.**

When we disconnect from our grief, we disconnect from ourselves. When we disconnect from ourselves, we disconnect from others and from the natural world. It is an insidious cycle of unnecessary suffering that pervades families, communities, cultures, and generations. By trying to circumvent suffering, we magnify it.

**Nature does not hurry,
yet everything is accomplished.**

—LAO TZU

A society that prevents a person from grieving as intensely as necessary and as long as necessary is a culture that promotes bypass.

• • •

There are two kinds of suffering: the suffering we run from because we are unwilling to face the truth of life and the suffering that comes when we're willing to stop running from the sorrows and difficulties of the world. The second kind of suffering will lead you to freedom.

—AJAHN CHAH

As we work with grief, there is no need to rush toward any goal, no need to move along to any particular destination. If we play any role at all, the most significant thing we can do is to help the bereaved feel the complete, unedited version of their particular story, in the context of their family and in the context of their culture.

• • •

If we cannot trust our ability to cope with the uninhibited rise and fall of grief, we will likely find it increasingly more difficult to tolerate our emotions, relying instead on the distractions that can easily become addictions when the intensity of grief flares up.

• • •

Like the rest of the natural world, grief has its own organic rhythm, its own pulse of change. All we have to do is feel it and give it space.

**Grief is a process
of expansion and contraction.**

> **All the beauty of this world is wet
> with the dew of tears.**
>
> —THEODOR HAECKER

The process of contraction and expansion in grief takes place over and over again. Within this model, contraction is not *wrong* or *bad*; contraction need not be halted or controlled. Contraction is necessary for expansion—and thus, contraction is itself part of expansion.

…

A contraction of grief occurs when our attention and energy are pulled inward, our surroundings made smaller perhaps because, in this particular moment, we feel overwhelmed. Feeling overwhelmed, we contract and tighten emotionally; we conserve our energy and attention, focusing intently on grief—and on self. In a moment of contraction, it feels as if our very survival may be in question. We may feel unsteady, unsafe, unheld; we may feel tenuous, desperate, fearful, and vulnerable. In such moments, we may curl up and hold our breath. In such moments, we feel the call to self-protect. We sense, on some level, that contraction will save us.

Expansion may come with the deep in-and-out breath, in a period of small, even minuscule, growth postcontraction. Allowing contraction to just be, in time we see it naturally ebbs, and the tightness loosens, we grow larger, and we become more willing to venture out and explore, to take risks, to open and unfold. And we find ourselves in a moment of trust, safety, curiosity, willingness, connectedness, belonging—and maybe even hope.

In previous moments, the contraction saved us; in this moment, the expansion will save us.

• • •

During contractions, it is essential to have others who can stand by us—so that when we arrive at the pinnacle of suffering, we can turn and look into the eyes of another's compassion and hold through to the other side. During expansion, it is essential to honor contraction too, to remember contraction and recall that we have endured many contractions—and will endure yet more.

Sometimes *being* in grief, or *being* weak, or *being* encased in a womb of pain was the only way I could continue to exist in any form.

The natural course of grief, as in the rest of nature, is contraction-expansion-contraction-expansion-contraction-expansion—perhaps endlessly. Our emotions *move*—within us, through us, and between us. Disintegration comes first. Reintegration follows. A contraction allows an expansion. This is the wisdom of the universe, the wisdom of your body, the wisdom of your heart.

. . .

I did not know that she could go away, and take our lives with her, yet leave our dull bodies behind. . . . How am I to comprehend this? How am I to have it? Why am I robbed, and who is benefited?
—MARK TWAIN

We do not experience grief without love, and we cannot experience the love without feeling grief. When we open our hearts to grief, over time, the delineation between the two states deliquesces. Our hearts open, because grief, like love, is a matter of the heart.

Unrestrained lamenting itself is a practice for being with grief.

Grief occupies the space between people. It has its place in the family, at the dinner table and on vacations, in pews and on porch swings. It occupies time and space, passed along from one generation to the next. Grief, like love, is open-ended. Yet in so many people, while love is welcomed and encouraged, grief is stifled and suppressed by fear.

I never knew grief felt so much like fear.

—C.S. LEWIS.

Grief can feel terrifying. And why would we not feel afraid? Deep in grief, we look up and see the reflection in our mirror is not our own, not us as we have previously known ourselves. We are changed, and we do not recognize the stranger we have become. We long for our old lives, our old selves; we crave meaning and belonging—we ache for them. The yearning is unquenchable. And that sense of emptiness propels us toward unsuccessful attempts to fill that person-shaped hole. The distractions we use to take us from our feelings are one way we try to sate that emptiness. The only alternative to distraction is *being with* grief—one painful, terrifying moment at a time.

...

We pause to *be with* grief, joining the rebellion against a hedonistic culture of happiness-at-all-costs and reclaiming our rightful feelings. We learn to *just be* without needing to tame, alter, or displace our emotions. This is radically countercultural, even revolutionary, when all other social forces merge to quell, overcome, and conquer grief. All the while, we renounce the ideas that happiness is something to pursue, a guarantee, an entitlement for every person, and that securing our own happiness is the preeminent purpose of life.

Fully inhabiting painful feelings helps us adjust to and accommodate them.

Grief is like the monster in my childhood closet: if I can muster the courage to get out of bed and turn on the light, I realize that he isn't so terrifying and may not even be who I believe he is. After going to look at him where he hides, I climb back into bed and confront his gaze again in the darkness. If I repeat this often enough, I even learn to trust him. I begin to understand that monster isn't separate from me. He is part of me, part of my mind.

• • •

It's typically American to equate healing with doing something. When we have a problem, we fix it, and we prefer to do it quickly. But fixing is not the same as healing; in fact it can easily get in the way of healing. . . Healing happens not through doing but through feeling.

—ELIO FRATTAROLI

> ### The healing from the pain
> ### is in the pain.
>
> —RUMI

The more we practice staying with the emotions that we think may overcome us, the more we trust our ability to fully inhabit grief. The more we inhabit it, the more comfortable we are staying and allowing it to move through us.

...

> Our holy place is holy still; our love is not diminished by absence or by pain. Death has but interrupted our loving, and I know I shall see you again, if the world lasts.
>
> —NANCY WOOD

...

Preoccupied and out of my body is not a way I want to live my life. So I decided that I would emulate the discalced Carmelites of the fifteenth century and hike barefoot down the trail. This practice, which I use about monthly, teaches me to stay present even when the present moment hurts. It teaches me that I can feel grateful for a cool, smooth stone on the path. It teaches me that I can avoid the cactus needles when I pay attention—and that rocks between my toes hurt. It teaches me that though I cannot always see around the next corner, I trust myself on this path. It teaches me that sometimes I can lean on the unexpected, like the titan juniper pine I'd walked past many times but never *really* saw. And it teaches me that I cannot provide shade for myself—only another being can provide shade for me. My barefoot hiking practice, rich in metaphors, is a compelling medium for me. While it's not for everyone, many others with whom I've worked have also integrated various aspects of barefootedness, even walking barefoot on their lawn or while playing golf, as part of their own practice. For me, walking barefoot is a way of being with grief.

• • •

Sharp knives seemed to cut her delicate feet, yet she hardly felt them—so deep was the pain in her heart.

—HANS CHRISTIAN ANDERSEN

• • •

Grief, particularly traumatic grief, is a wound to the self. When we are deeply wounded, we *must* turn our focus to the injured place in order to survive and become who we will become in the aftermath of catastrophe.

> **Wherever we are in our grief journey, *pausing* causes us to land on the self. Grief is love turned into an eternal missing.**
>
> —ROSAMUND LUPTON

Ultimately, when we take good care of ourselves, we are better able to take care of others. Far from being selfish, in a way self-care in grief is heroic. This is the place of heart-turned-inward.

· · ·

We will move, vacillating between self and other, heart-in and heart-out, over time. What this means for grievers is that we may have re-grieving days, days when acutely experienced grief reemerges months, years, or decades later on a special day, holidays, or without any particular cue or prompt. On re-grieving days, grief moves to the foreground again, and we may feel weepier than usual, tenderhearted, and vulnerable.

A Letter to Myself

Dear One,

Please remember to

Have a good cry when you need one.
Drink plenty of water.
Connect with compassionate others.
Accept and embrace emotions without clinging to them,
    even the good ones.

Find the sun every day.
Learn to love solitude.
Serve others every opportunity you can.
Sleep seven hours a night.
Eat clean.
Play dirty (get in the mud, walk barefoot, sweat).
Remember your precious dead.
Feel grateful but don't force gratitude.
Notice nature.
Try new things.
Pray and/or meditate.
Find your special song.
Seek out those who made a difference in your life and
    tell them. Build bridges between people.
Take a media break.

Treat yourself to a day of comfort.
Rescue an animal.
Buy a stranger a cup of coffee or tea, or lunch.
    Anonymously. Start over again.

With love, I'm trying,
YOURSELF

**Self-care is crucial
for those who are grieving.
Its necessity is nonnegotiable.
Self-care is not a selfish act;
it is an act of generosity
for self and others.**

A way to create your own self-practice is to break self-care down into categories. I suggest the following broad areas to attend to: self-expression, self-awareness, connection and interconnection, physicality, and kindness. Self-expression is about the ways in which we show our feelings. Self-awareness is about the ways in which we begin to pay attention, notice, and listen deeply to all aspects of self. Connection and interconnection are about the ways in which we are present with others, animals, nature, the world, and even ourselves. Physicality is about tending to our bodily health, paying attention to sleep, nutrition, exercise, dance, and even, when ready, play. Kindness is about bringing love to others, and we cannot bring love to others without bringing it back around to ourselves—it's a symbiosis and a wonderful way to care for our own hearts.

• • •

I wish I could show you when you are lonely or in darkness the astonishing light of your own being.

—HAFIZ

• • •

To embrace suffering culminates in greater empathy, the capacity to feel what it is like for the other to suffer, which is the ground for unsentimental compassion and love.

—STEPHEN BATCHELOR

• • •

There is no question that, for many, grief and the sense of isolation and loneliness amplifies during special occasions, like baby showers, graduations or weddings, and on holidays.

She was a genius of sadness, immersing herself in it, separating its numerous strands, appreciating its subtle nuances. She was a prism through which sadness could be divided into its infinite spectrum.

—JONATHAN SAFRAN FOER

• • •

Self-care means attending to the body, mind, and heart in the wake of loss, but we must be careful not to let this become yet another form of distraction—like any other distraction that mindlessly takes us away from painful feelings.

Self-care also means saying *no* when necessary. When grieving, we need to give ourselves permission to put our own needs first for a while.

All things become potential teachers when we are paying attention. When this happens, we begin seeing things we've never seen, perceiving even minutia in the natural world and noticing that the rainbow and the storm show up in the same sky. When the darkness of grief descends, our eyes need time to adjust to this condition—to begin to see subtler and more dimly lit presences.

> **Always go too far because that is where you will find the truth.**
> —ALBERT CAMUS

Practicing attentive self-awareness, we may start to see that there is life in a planted seed working hard under the soil. And we may notice that the trees less likely to break are those that are able to sway with the wind. We may discern that the easy path isn't always the right path. And everyone and everything can become our teacher. Children and strangers teach us. Animals teach us. When we are truly awake, even an ordinary moment teaches us something.

• • •

Grieving itself is a learning process. We learn so much about ourselves in grief—perhaps more than we could ever want to know. The more I learn about grief, the less I fear it, and the more I felt rooted in myself.

> The world breaks us all,
> and afterward some are stronger
> in those broken places.
> —ERNEST HEMINGWAY

As the seasons change, we are reminded of the losses of winter. Trees lose their leaves. Nature loses her color. The warmth loses its hold on the world. And we miss things. We miss the green leaves and the kaleidoscopic colors and the warmth of the sun on our faces. Nature teaches us about loss every passing year. Yet nothing can prepare us for some losses, those catastrophic losses, in our lives. And although the leaves of our trees may return when we are ready, our trees are never the same trees again.

Grieving is also a process of adaptation. We find ways to adjust to the life we never expected or wanted.

Grieving hones our intuition. We are listening more deeply, and our senses, in ways different from before our beloved's death, are sharper, the result of having practiced penetrating awareness of self and surroundings. Sometimes we learn to trust our intuition.

Turning toward what you deeply love saves you.

—RUMI

Grief calls for us
to give ourselves back to it.
To remember.
To reclaim.
To re-grieve.
And for all those things,
even when they sting,
I am thankful.

Cultivating a practice of surrendering means that we intentionally approach grief over and over.

Our awareness of grief's influence is heightened: the presence of our beloved dead's absence undeniable. We come to appreciate that this immense present grief is here because of another period in time when we were together with them. And that time, that precious time, belongs to us.

...

Employers, neighbors, family, friends, and concerned others begin to send messages—both subtle and overt— urging us to resume life as usual. But life is anything but usual after the one we love has died. We are changed beings even if we have resumed some semblance of a "new normal."

I have faith in nights.
—RAINER MARIA RILKE

Being with grief, we stretch our bodies and hearts until the point of pain. As with any stretch, maybe we back off just a little, out of necessity and self-care. Over time, as we hold the stretch, reaching our edge, we learn to wait. In this surrender, our muscles give in to the pose, they soften. As we repeat the exercise, we surrender more and more deeply into the stretch. Friends, colleagues, family members may call to us to abandon the stretch, because to them it no longer feels necessary.

With practice, we can learn how to balance the things of the living with our beloved dead.

The conscious choice not to relegate grief to the sidelines where it will never be seen, but rather to give it a place in our lives where it will be cared for and remembered is courageous. And a heart that has been expanded by suffering has the capacity to hold even more love.

**Disconnection from grief fragments
our already fragile identity.**

By re-grieving and remembering, we discover the mysterious power of staying in the stretch, remaining connected to both the beauty of loving and the pain of having lost. Surrendering requires our steadfast commitment to stand up and turn *toward* grief while living in a culture obsessed with ushering grief, scorned, out the door.

. . .

The invitation to surrender to grief is about the middle path, straddling both worlds—life and death—without clinging or avoiding, and it comes with both pure love and pain.

**Protecting the intimate connection
to our beloved dead can be, for us,
an elixir of life.**

But there was no need to be ashamed of tears, for tears bore witness that a man had the greatest of courage, the courage to suffer.

—VIKTOR FRANKL

• • •

The idea that grief incrementally weakens by the mere passage of time has not been my truth. Nor would I wish it to be. It isn't how much time has passed that counts. It's what we—and others around us—do with that time.

• • •

I decided early that I would not be willing to fragment parts of myself in order to make me—or those around me—comfortable. And, by allowing myself to be with grief, to bear its weight, to carry it, I have become stronger. Eventually I became strong enough to help others carry their grief.

• • •

When we remember our beloved dead, we bridge the gap of space and time between us and them and bring them back into the whole of our reality.

**Seeking to live without grief,
we diminish our ability
to feel truly content.**

Over time, as I kept stretching, kept lifting grief's weight, I grew stronger and more flexible—becoming better able to carry grief in all its myriad shape-shifting forms. The weight I needed to bear never changed—only my ability to carry it.

...

Those we love deeply who have died are part of our identity; they are a part of our biography. We feel that love in the marrow of our bones. There is a lingering call to remember them that, though sometimes muted by the chaos of the world, never fades away.

**Surrendering to grief is an act
of necessary courage.**

The thing about grief is that there isn't a place or time at which we arrive once-and-for-all at peace or healing or completion.

• • •

Grief is a process, an unending long and winding road. The landscape changes as we travel the distance, some parts of the path barren and some more beautiful—but it's the same road. And grief itself is the destination: at every moment of our grief, we are arriving.

Let's stop making deals for a safe passage.
—JOYCE WELLWOOD

Grief is not a medical disorder to be cured.
Grief is not a spiritual crisis to be resolved.
Grief is not a social woe to be addressed.
Grief is, simply, a matter of the heart—to be felt.

> **Though we encounter it as suffering, grief is in fact an affirmation.**
>
> —LEON WIESELTIER

Grief violates convention: it is raw, primal, seditious, chaotic, writhing, and most certainly uncivilized. Yet grief is an affirmation of human passion, and only those who are apathetic, who stonewall love, who eschew intimacy can escape grief's pull. No intervention and no interventionist can "cure" our grief. And we are not broken—we are brokenhearted.

. . .

Be skeptical of the advice you internalize.

. . .

Find those who are willing to join you and walk with you nonjudgmentally.

What restraint or limit should there be to grief for one so dear?

—HORACE

Steer clear of those who claim to have a cure for your grief. Surround yourself instead with those who admit they have no answers but who will enter into the realm of unknowing with you. Seek others doing real soul work and join hands with them, your tribe.

· · ·

Listen deeply and you will recognize other citizens of the country of sorrow. They are many, and they are beautiful.

· · ·

The pain is there; when you close one door on it, it knocks to come in somewhere else.

—IRVIN D. YALOM

Finding specific words for our present-moment experiences of the loss can be helpful.

The word *surrender* means to give back something or yield ourselves over to something. In the context of grieving, we give ourselves over to grief. Anything that takes us from our routine of life into the sacred space of intentional grief can be part of a surrendering practice.

• • •

Here we are all in one place. The wants and wounds of the human race. Despair and hope sit face to face when you come in from the cold.

—Carrie Newcomer

When we learn to be with grief, our own hearts soften and open.

When our hearts soften, we also begin to more clearly see others' pain.

As we cultivate a practice of surrendering, of being with suffering, we will see that our own circle of relatability—that sense of oneness with the other—widens. Our own pain gives us access to an inexhaustible wellspring of compassion.

. . .

There is no heart more whole than a broken one.
—THE KOTZKER REBBE

. . .

Rather than abating or diminishing us, grief holds the possibility of creating space to expand our hearts to the paradox of coexisting pain and love—for ourselves and others. We engage this process by feeling—and remembering.

. . .

It is one's duty to love those we do not see.
—SØREN KIERKEGAARD

**In remembering our beloved dead,
we hold open their place in our hearts.**

Remembering our dead epitomizes the most unselfish, freest, and most faithful type of love—a love willing to suffer for itself, so that it can continue to exist. It is unselfish because it is unrequited; our calling to our beloved dead cannot be reciprocated in the ways we so desire. It is freest because there is no coercion or obligation to continue loving the dead; it can only be an act of choice. It is faithful because it requires devotion; for neither affection, nor strength, nor kindness can be returned from one who has died.

**In remembering our beloved dead,
we love faithfully and with
unwavering intention.**

The plea for closeness to our dead can always be heard—if we are still, if we listen. When we ignore that call for too long, we fragment. When we remember them, we bring the whole of their existence back into our hearts.

> **Between grief and nothing,**
> **I will take grief.**
> —WILLIAM FAULKNER

There were times I felt like I was catapulted into the dark, deep water where waves of pain crashed down upon me relentlessly. Grief, like a powerful riptide, pulled me into its black water and carried me, against my will, far from the familiar shore. I could no longer see my home, my life, or my self between the surges that hammered me. I fought for the slightest glimpse of sky. The waves persisted. They tumbled me, over and over and over, disorienting and confusing me. Deeper and deeper, the riptide pulled me under water. I was gasping for air.

I fought the grief, but it was much stronger—I could not win. Then grief whispered into my ear with a firm tenderness, "Surrender—you won't die from the pain." And for a brief moment, I heeded. Surprised, I reached the surface for a desperate pocket of air only to panic and resist again, plunging myself back under the dark waters of grief that filled my lungs.

I knew I would not survive unless I surrendered. And so I surrendered. I relaxed into the tide, and it guided me to the surface, carrying me to shore—familiar yet not—where it would release me.

**The gift of surrender:
a deepened sense of authenticity
and trust in oneself.**

We must entrust ourselves to both the calm and raging motions of grief. We must learn to be patient with its unpredictability, patient with its bitterness and wreckage, and in exchange, slowly grief will be kinder. We can become cautious comrades with grief at first. One day, perhaps, devoted partners in remembering.

• • •

When we are caught in a riptide or overtaken by a shadow, we can trust that this moment will pass and we will regain the ability to breathe again—at least for a while.

Love doesn't die; people do.

—MERRIT MALLOY

We do know how to remember, we know how to call back those we love into our hearts—even when those memories come with deep longing and sadness. When we remember our beloved dead, they are with us.

Ritual is the antidote to helplessness.

—SUKIE MILLER

Ritual serves to honor the contents of our hearts. Every society has rituals associated with death and grief. They serve the function of *connection maintenance*—helping us feel closer to our loved one who has died. Emotional expression revives a sense of control, helps us feel meaning, and underpins communal structures within which we are better able to cope with our losses.

Rituals can be large and well-planned (organizing a candle lighting, a toy drive, or a gathering to remember) or spontaneous and small (microrituals such as saying "good morning" to your loved one, burning incense, or praying and meditating). Microrituals can include attention to items of remembrance such as a photograph, a favorite symbol or song, handwritten notes, and other personal items. They can also include sacrificing something we value or want, from social engagement to physical comfort. In addition to helping others who are hungry, about once a month, I fast for an entire day to connect with the feeling of being hungry.

Microrituals can go on for decades— indefinitely even.

Ritual acts, whether public or private, large-scale or small, are a means to unmask feelings of love and pain and to prompt others toward connection. Microrituals are a purposeful means of invoking our beloved dead's presence in our day-to-day lives.

Through art and ceremony, through narrative and creation, through act and speech and silence, through symbols and withstanding pain, rituals and microrituals help us remember. And in that way, they help us to love.

• • •

I intend to breathe my way through conflict,
To breathe my way through the great risks,
To breathe my way through the ebb and flow of grief,
To breathe my way through the muck and mire of life,
To breathe my way through dark disappointments.
I intend to be with my true self,
To listen for what is beneath the stillness,
To see the lingering pain of others,
To bow before the great teachers—children and nature,
To love all things more fully.
I intend to open my arms and my heart to the world,
remembering that we belong to each other

We cannot help another without also helping ourselves.

Nothing can make up for the absence of someone we love, and it would be wrong to try and find a substitute; we must simply hold out and see it through. That sounds very hard at first, but at the same time it is a great consolation. It remains unfilled, preserves the bonds between us.

—DIETRICH BONHOEFFER

• • •

Compassion is more than just a feeling. Sometimes compassion means taking action, making connections. And it is precisely our own grief, our own pain, that enables us to connect to the suffering of others. Beyond merely being with grief, we must also *do with* it. In doing with grief, grief is not gone, or forgotten, or recovered from. Grief remains our partner, our companion—the source of our compassionate action in the world. When we *do with* grief, grief is being lived openly, honestly. Grief becomes ennobling.

Our loss is precious to us because it can wake us up to love, and to loving action.

—NORMAN FISCHER

Compassion arises when we yield to our own pain instead of evading it, when we allow our hearts to remain open and gracious. Yet no part of the grief journey can ever be rushed—including meaning-seeking and compassionate action. Even these can be subverted into bypass to hasten and move away from grief.

. . .

The redemptive potential of fully inhabited grief actualizes when our deepening self-awareness merges with our broadening other-awareness and swallows, in oneness, the space between. This synthesis of inward and outward, self and other, expresses the relationship we have with our loved ones who have died. We meet them inside our hearts, and then we find ways to carry their spirit into the world. Suffering endured becomes compassion expressed. Grieving becomes giving. Pain becomes wisdom.

The road of sorrow is not easy.

While grieving the death of someone loved will last a lifetime, if we are able to remain honestly close to our original wound, being with it and surrendering to it, we can experience a kind of transcendence, a transfiguration. Meaningful moments arise in continuous rhythm. Our hearts are completely, lastingly broken open, turned outward toward others, even others quite unlike us. We begin to realize oneness in an undeniably personal way.

· · ·

When we cannot hold in our arms our loved ones who've died, we hold them in our hearts. This is *being with* grief.

When we have been too long in the absence of their song, we turn toward their whispers. This is *surrendering to* grief.

When we cannot look into their eyes, we tender their vision of compassion where it's most needed. This is *doing with* grief.

· · ·

> Before you know kindness
> as the deepest thing inside,
> you must know sorrow
> as the other deepest thing.
> —NAOMI SHIHAB NYE

· · ·

It is in knowing suffering, in all its darkest places and with all its most harrowing faces, that we are brought to a place of fierce compassion for others and, perhaps one day, for ourselves.

· · ·

At some times, the turn toward compassionate action unfurls so slowly. At other times, the calling is more precipitous, a tsunami in response to quakes of fully inhabited grief. And this is how our world will change.

· · ·

Those who have deeply suffered understand life in ways other cannot: they know the only way to attain authentic and lasting contentment is to turn our hearts outward in service to those who are suffering as we have suffered. We are present with life because we are present with death. We know joy and peace because we are present with grief and suffering.

· · ·

Since her first grief had brought her fully to birth and wakefulness in this world, an unstinting compassion had moved in her, like a live stream flowing deep underground by which she knew herself and others and the world.

—WENDELL BERRY

{ 74 }

It is compassion that will help to heal this world.

Our task as humans is to extend compassion to all beings, large and small, like us and unlike us, those in mourning and those in pain—and to extend compassion to our own selves.

Compassion toward oneself can manifest in compassion toward others.

And compassion toward others can express compassion toward oneself.

...

The first peace, which is the most important, is that which comes within the souls of people when they realize their relationship, their oneness with the universe and all its powers, and when they realize that at the center of the universe dwells the Great Spirit, and that this center is really everywhere, it is within each of us.

—BLACK ELK

It is the bereaved who can heal our world.

Repressed grief ravages individuals and dismantles families; its tragic effects seep like groundwater into communities and societies. And the emotional economics of grief denied its rightful place are grim.

• • •

"Did you see Death go by with my little child?" asked the mother. "Yes," said the blackthorn bush. "But I shall not tell you which way he went unless you warm me against your heart—I am freezing to death; I am stiff with ice." The mother pressed the blackthorn bush against her heart to warm it, and the thorns stabbed so deep into her flesh that great drops of red blood flowed. So warm was the mother's heart that the blackthorn bush blossomed and put forth green leaves on that dark winter's night. And it told her the way to go.

—HANS CHRISTIAN ANDERSEN

• • •

After all, when a stone is dropped into a pond, the water continues quivering even after the stone has sunk to the bottom.

—ARTHUR GOLDEN

. . .

Transgenerational trauma, also called historical trauma, is real and exceedingly potent. It can be seen in family systems and in cultural systems. The deep psychological wounds and near obliteration of tribes; the killing of countless native children and adults; the subjugation, enslavement, torture, oppression, involuntary diaspora, and kidnapping of children from their families and tribes are a calamitous trauma that has been burned into the minds and hearts of those who suffered at the hands of European occupiers and their descendants.

A little drop of love in an ocean of pain can sustain countless beings.

Like trauma, the effects of "no time for grief"—of denying grief's existence—are addictions, abuse, and violence, often against the vulnerable: children, women, the elderly, and animals. These effects touch all of us.

• • •

The alternative to repressing grief is to fully inhabit it. When we have learned to fully inhabit our grief, we awaken to the suffering in others. We recognize harm in all relations, human-to-human, adult-to-child, adult-to-animal, child-to-animal. And then, having awakened to our own suffering and the suffering of others, we can begin to take action, when and where we can, that serve to diminish suffering rather than amplify it.

• • •

We must reach out to others less fortunate and show compassion, because to receive compassion, even if over time and slowly, is to know compassion. And to know compassion, even if from ourselves, is to be able to show compassion.

• • •

Time past and time future
What might have been and what has been
Point to one end, which is always present.
—T.S. ELIOT

**Grief is like broth.
The flavors of all our griefs merge
and become one flavor.**

Grief is synergistic, the whole growing greater than the sum of the individual parts. This truth reminds us to stop questioning and doubting the waves of grief that were hitting us and just allow our emotions to be what they were.

**Grief transforms from
the individual into
the collective.**

No one is as capable of gratitude as one who has emerged from the kingdom of night.
—ELIE WIESEL

I know some painfully learned truths:
I know life is fleeting,
and sometimes even children die.
I know that life promises us nothing.
I know that forgiveness does not come easily in grief,
especially toward myself.
I know that no drink, no pill, no religion, and no book
can save me from suffering.
I know that people we love can and do die
and that no one is exempt.
I know that control is an illusion.
I know that one day, one year, ten years, twenty years,
    and fifty years
is never enough time with those we love.
I know that there is nothing we can trade,
nothing we can barter, nothing we can give
to negotiate our loved ones back to life
—not even offering ourselves in their place.
And I know the secret that life goes on,
but it's never the same.

**We are all connected by
suffering and loss.**

When we remain conscious of our susceptibility to suffering, we can notice the constant hum of fear, a rumble of insatiable terror, and we can remind ourselves how normal it is to be afraid to lose again, to want some type of guarantee or protection against more trauma and grief. And we must know this is unattainable.

————————

Unless we manage to avoid love, we will not avoid grief.

————————

Your tears are not only your tears; my tears are not only my tears.

Imagine that the tears we shed will make their way into a creek near our homes, which leads to the river miles away, which flows into the great ocean of sorrow. Other creeks and other rivers have carried to the same ocean the sorrows of many other mothers and fathers and sisters and brothers and grandparents and lovers and spouses and friends and aunts and uncles and neighbors and strangers who have also grieved, who have also deeply mourned.

The myth of separateness is an illusion to keep us safe from vulnerability; separateness is a mirage that stifles realization of our connectedness.

...

Every tear you shed and all the countless tears shed by myriad others throughout time and space have become drops in the vast oceanic story of loving and grieving.

The pain of grief is legitimately ours.

Being with grief can be terrifyingly painful, yet when we live our grief honestly, it has the mysterious power to deepen the meaning of our lives. This is the gift-curse of grief.

...

We may never be able to make sense of why our loved one died—but when we fully inhabit our grief, over time, we can begin to make sense of why we're still alive. Compassion for others, when we are ready to rise from our knees and stand again, is one of the few things that help keep our hearts open toward a world where those we so deeply love can—and do—die.

· · ·

Every moment is a secret cache.
Each breath is an offering.
And every increment of time is irreplaceable.
The only thing for which life offers even a fleeting
 guarantee
is this moment—right here and right now.
This is all we have, all we ever have.
It is both absolving and terrifying.

Compassion for others can help us make sense of our lives.

Amid great and crushing grief, we don't need to bear a lifetime of unbearable grief all at once. All we ever need to do, all we ever need to endure, is one moment at a time. Just this moment. And this one. And this one. In this way, one second at a time, we can build the emotional muscle needed to bear the weight of absence for one more second, one more hour, one more day. It comes in time.

As a nation, I surmise that we do not grieve enough. And in many respects, I would say that many of our issues that we are challenged with in society are a direct result of a lack of grieving.

—DR. BERNICE KING

• • •

Let yourself feel, even when it hurts; especially when it hurts. It's part of being real and alive. Reclaim every inch of your emotions as yours. Nothing will be as liberating as that.

• • •

No task on earth, perhaps, will be as worthy as when you bring all the parts of you back to their home.

• • •

Oh grief,
I remember the day we met,
so unexpectedly.

I turned the corner of life and there you were

shivering and lost,
on the barren ground,
a fallen bird with a broken wing.

As so I picked you up and held you, cupped
    tenderly in my palms.

I brought you home into my heart, though others
    said I should not.

I hand-fed you each time you cried out in pangs,
and protected you from more harm.

I made a nest for you, safe and warm, to rest
until your aching bones mended,
on their own accord.

And when you were ready,
when you were strong enough to fly,
I set you free
into the world,
so that you might bless others with your songs of
    beauty,

songs of the broken-winged ones,

knowing always
that you were first mine
but that I couldn't possibly keep those songs
to only myself.

Our time together may have been limited, but our love . . .
our love is timeless, endless.

————◆————

We only deeply mourn what we deeply love.

————◆————

We can, for a time, hide from our trauma and grief as if they don't exist. But we cannot hide from the *consequences* of hiding from our trauma and grief.

• • •

> After you died
> all things changed.
> Dust collected around the house
> payments went unpaid
> and calls unreturned
> casseroles went uneaten
> teeth unbrushed
> plants unwatered
> thank-you cards unmailed.

After you died
the smell of rain disappeared
birds lost their melody
stones turned to ash
and clouds to concrete
the sky surrendered its blue
grasses withered and trees fell.

After you died
a part of me did, too
and what remained
collapsed under the weight
of your constant absence
and all things changed.

And, I realized that all things had to change
because my world could not remain
the same without you.

Sameness would not sufficiently honor
the holiness of your mark upon my heart
the longing for every part of you
even parts I would never know.
After you died
all things changed.
All things changed
except my love for you.

We begin to realize that there is no time or place when we won't feel the density of our loved ones' absence. Feeling this, touching this, is the place where we can meet our beloved ones over and over, through the course of our lives, in spite of—indeed, *because of*—our deep grief and never-ending love.

Our grief cannot and should not be governed by others.

Your grief is a holy land that belongs to you, not psychological colonizers. Listen to that small still voice in the center of your own broken heart and take back what is yours. Listen to that sacred knowing deep in your soul that tells you this pain has its place and time, and that your beloved's absence calls for such protestations. When others judge your grief, reject that judgment if it offends your heart.

• • •

Tenderly, I now touch all things knowing
one day we will part.
—HAFIZ

Here and there.
Then and now.
Yesterday, today, tomorrow.
I am yours and
You are mine.
No one and nothing can take that from the
center of my heart

· · ·

Real isn't how you are made. It's a thing that happens to you. Sometimes it hurts, but when you are Real you don't mind being hurt. It doesn't happen all at once. You become. Once you are Real you can't be ugly, except to people who don't understand. Once you are Real you can't become unreal again. It lasts for always.

—MARGERY WILLIAMS,
THE VELVETEEN RABBIT

· · ·

When others bypass, dismiss, ignore, minimize, and shame our grief, it exaggerates the distance between us and them, between those suffering and those not suffering. And that is, perhaps, what some seek: a sense of false protection by rationalizing why this tragedy happened to us and not them. Some feel protected from loss by using feigned spirituality, insincere happiness, and chronic superficiality, fearing the place where humans most intimately connect heart-to-heart: in the dark abyss of the indelible absence of those we so love who have died.

Sometimes, we just want others to see us as we are. Some days we are not okay—we just need others to make space for that, and for us.

We can also experience something bigger than grief, one day, if our hearts allow. And that bigger thing is ineffable. It contains many more layers than just the raw grief, and it is very hard to put into words.

What better use for a broken heart than to bow deeply to the broken heart of another.

If others cannot imagine why you're grieving so much for so long, remind them to be thankful that they do not understand.

----◆----

**The work of grieving
is hallowed ground,
deserving of our pause,
our recognition,
and hands pressed
together at our hearts.**

----◆----

Life does not accommodate you; it shatters you.
Every seed destroys its container,
or else there would be no fruition.
—FLORIDA SCOTT-MAXWELL

Beneath anger, grief; beneath grief, love.
Beyond that, the clear blue sky.

—ZEN POEM

Grief is always in the mix—coexisting with joy, love, contentment, and all the other emotions that others mistakenly assume indicates we are "over" grief. That is nonsense. Integration is what's called for, not "getting over" grief. There is no "getting over." Integration happens in the center of our hearts when we are loved and supported by others, when we remember and feel held in that remembering, and when we allow ourselves to feel.

Just one day,
one moment,
one breath at a time
is what we need to endure.

They may tell you to move on.
They may tell you it's not normal to grieve this long.
They may tell you it's part of God's plan.
Your shattering makes them uneasy.
Vulnerable.
Some may avoid you, others may pity you.
But this is your grief.
Your grief is your own.

You have earned every single tear you shed.
You own this pain,
Even on days you wish it weren't so.
Don't let anyone take it from you.
Through the grief—and the love—
hold your head high,
even when you are suffering most.
Perhaps especially when you are suffering most.
Surround yourself with loving others.
Give yourself time to feel.

And one day, suffering endured
will become compassion expressed.

• • •

Let us show compassion toward our fellow human beings. Let us show compassion toward the fellow animals who share this planet. Let us show compassion toward the Mother, our earth, who holds us all in abundant stead. Let us not forget that we ourselves will—very soon—be gone from this place. Let us strive to leave morsels of compassion that, collectively, will diminish violence, cruelty, and stupor. In that way, we will have done our small part in a very big way.

I live a full and meaningful life not in spite of grief but because of grief.

You know those grief-laden days when every song is theirs, when around every corner is a reminder of their absence? You know those "grief hangovers" when every sound is the wrong sound, nothing tastes the same, nothing is right in the world, and even breathing is painful?

When I'm in that place, I try to remember that it's all because of a vast love, a love that is extraordinary, beyond this world. I try to remember that all this immense grief is simply because of that moment in time when we were together and that that moment belongs only to us. Then I see I would not trade those moments or that love for anything, not even the promise of abated grief.

Don't let others tell you how to grieve any more than you'd allow others to tell you how to love.

It is not half so important to know as to feel.
—RACHEL CARSON

• • •

When someone intimates that I shouldn't feel grief for "so long," I am reminded: "There is only one you. There is only one me. There is only one us. And that is worthy of my grief."

• • •

Forgive me, distant wars, for bringing flowers home.
Forgive me, open wounds, for pricking my finger.
—WISŁAWA SZYMBORSKA

The holiest of all holidays are those
Kept by ourselves in silence and apart;
The secret anniversaries of the heart.
—HENRY WADSWORTH LONGFELLOW

Each day, when your goneness comes, again and again,
and your deadness continues to spurn negotiation
what remains is the ordinary
presence of your absence
a vacancy that gorges on longing
for you, for us, for what should have been.

There exists no meaning—
other than this complex grief
and this simple love I refuse to conceal.

. . .

I mourn every moment without you: the sad moments
and even the happy moments, and the moments that are
neither. I mourn for every part of every day you're missing.
I mourn your absence even when I'm unaware I'm mourning. And this is the truth of love.

Crying is one of the highest devotional songs. One who knows crying, knows spiritual practice. If you can cry with a pure heart, nothing else compares to such a prayer.

—KRIPALVANANDA

•••

At first, my body whispered to me, "Pay attention."

Then my body gently admonished, "Please, hear my call."

Then it yelled, "Hear me!"

And then, when all other options were off the table, my body forced me to do what I should have done out of self-love: it brought me into rest and stillness through sickness.

"If only you'd listened the first time," my body whispered again.

And I learned, finally, that caring for myself was simply not the "option" I thought it was.

**Grief is not monochromatic.
Grief, when fully lived is,
just like nature itself, kaleidoscopic
and intensely hued.**

For Those Who Grieve

May you rise strong out of the ashes
with the fire of loss in your belly
and the tenderness of love guiding your heart.

May you carry that love with the ferocity of a warrior,
a love of extraordinary force that knows no boundaries,
no limits.

May you bravely face the questions of others
who do not and cannot know,
and with a mighty voice speak your truth,
and with quivering legs stand tall
and despite the fear in your heart,
may you turn toward your own sage soul with reluctant trust.

May you feel held by the arms of others
who have known this loss through history.

And may the wisdom of the ages carry you in solidarity
through all the dark nights you will face.

And when you fall, may you fall back gently into the shadow
with compassion, courage,
and the resolve to rise again.

And again. And again.

Loneliness is one of the most common emotional experiences of those who grieve. And it's no wonder. We live in a world so obsessed with feeling "good," with toxic positivity, and forcing "happiness" that often any authentic expression of sadness or despair is quickly and abruptly judged and marginalized as pathology. Letting grieving people grieve can diminish their loneliness.

• • •

My heart shattered
broken into millions of pieces,
The day you died.

And because there was nothing else to do,
I let those shattered pieces land
softly in the world.

And when I could, again, breathe,
with a regular rhythm,
I noticed, quietly, painfully
the places where splintered shards of my heart
came to a rest.

Somewhere amid the fragments of your too-brief life,
reflecting ineluctable grief, I know
that your love is, by comparison,
so much more vast and infinite than my shattering.

Mental anguish always results from the avoidance of legitimate suffering.

—STEFAN MOLYNEUX

• • •

One day, the grief makes space for something else as well, in its own time and way. Something changes, subtly but profoundly. We learn to hold both grief and a kind of pure, albeit reluctant, joy in the expansion, the way that space holds both the sun and the moon.

• • •

When you remember me, it means that you have carried something of who I am with you, that I have left some mark of who I am on who you are. It means that you can summon me back to your mind even though countless years and miles may stand between us. It means that if we meet again, you will know me. It means that even after I die, you can still see my face and hear my voice and speak to me in your heart.

—FREDERICK BUECHNER

What can we do in their absence, when life feels incomplete?

We can protest the fact they are not here. And grieve.

We can remember them. And grieve.

We can speak their names. And grieve.

We can see their light rise with the sun. And grieve.

We can imagine them walking with us. And grieve.

We can miss them more than words can express. And grieve.

We can live our lives to honor them, to make them proud.

And we can grieve.

We grieve.

And we love.

Life goes on,

but it doesn't

because nothing is ever the same.

Death has taken from us,

but it hasn't

because it cannot take

what never dies:

Love.

Closure is for doors and cupboards and windows, not for emotions, particularly not for grief. The concept of closure does not apply to grief.

The cost of trying to close or enclose grief is high: addiction; inauthentic emotions; disconnection from self, from others, from the earth and nature.

When we are suffering, we don't need more barriers from one heart to another. We need connection, compassion, and love. We need to feel upheld in our grief. We need others to accept our sadness and love us however we show up in the world.

So, instead of worrying about how to make grieving people find "closure," let's worry about helping those who aren't grieving find compassion. In that way, we needn't worry about closing—we are, rather, in a state of opening, unfolding, and becoming.

> I search for threads of you
> everywhere I go
> I find you in the small crevices of life
> and in the bottomless canyons
> I find you in the ordinarily beige moments
> and in conspicuous beauty
> I long for morsels of your presence
> in everything I do . . .
> even when it means feeling bloodied
> by the shards of grief
> and the breathtakingly painful
> presence of your absence
> I will always look for you
> and I will always find you
> as long as I can love.

Epilogue: A Benediction

I wish for you to be loved unconditionally through grief's loneliest moments, when you go into their room and lay on their bed, when you find a strand of their hair in an old brush, when you simply, purely miss them with every part of your being or when you find yourself listening for the tiny whisper of that irreplaceable voice and laugh.

I wish for you strength to allow weakness, to reach out for the hand of another when you are vulnerable.

When the magnitude of the implacable loss has you in its grip, I wish for you the tenderest of grief's touches born of inimitable love.

In your darkest moments of the deepest pain and longing, I wish for you the kindness of others who will join you there, meet you in your sorrow, and remember with you.

I wish for you—and for me, and for us all—to embody this compassion toward all others, toward all beings, and to unfurl our love for those who have died into the world so they will touch others through us.

ACKNOWLEDGMENTS

Gassho to all those who have shared their precious children, siblings, parents, and partners with me through twenty-five years of doing this work. I carry a piece of each of your stories tucked in my heart.

. . .

Gassho to my editor, Josh Bartok, and Wisdom Publications for believing in the importance of grieving honestly.

. . .

Gassho to all the rescued animals of Selah Carefarm who have regained trust in the world and allowed me to offer compassion and love and who now give compassion and love to grieving hearts from around the world.

. . .

And gassho to all the animals around the world who, too, know what it is to grieve, to fear, to lose, to feel lonely, and to be separated from family. One day, humankind will awaken to your pain and will see the beauty of your existence. Until then, I will fight for you.

• • •

Gassho to my beloved parents, John and Jo, who died many years ago, and to my beautiful baby daughter, my greatest teacher of all time, Cheyenne. I will miss you until my last dying breath.

• • •

And finally, I stand in stead for all of you who will know grief today, tomorrow, and next year and who will read these words. May you be held in ways that help you bear the unbearable, one day, perhaps, helping another.

Index of Proper Names

About the Author

Dr. Joanne Cacciatore is the author of *Bearing the Unbearable: Love, Loss, and the Heartbreaking Path of Grief*. Her newborn daughter died on July 27, 1994, and that single tragic moment catapulted her unwillingly onto the reluctant path of traumatic grief. For more than two decades, she's devoted herself to counseling traumatically bereaved people from around the world. She's an associate professor and director of the Graduate Certificate in Trauma and Bereavement program at Arizona State University. In addition, she's the founder of an international nongovernmental organization, the MISS Foundation, dedicated to support to families experiencing the death of a child at any age and from any cause. Cacciatore is ordained with the Zen Garland Order and runs the Selah Carefarm for the traumatically bereaved, just outside Sedona, Arizona. The carefarm is a transformative and therapeutic community that connects almost forty animals rescued from abuse and torture with grieving families from around the world.

She is an acclaimed public speaker and provides expert consulting and witness services in the area of traumatic loss. Her research has been published in peer-reviewed journals such as *The Lancet*, *The BMJ*, *Health and Place*, and *Death Studies*, among others.

She received her PhD from the University of Nebraska–Lincoln and her master's and bachelor's degrees in psychology from Arizona State University. Her work has been featured in major media sources such as *Newsweek* magazine, the *New York Times*, the *Boston Globe*, CNN, National Public Radio, BBC, and the *Los Angeles Times*. She has been the recipient of many regional and national awards for her compassionate work and service to people suffering traumatic grief.

A longtime animal advocate, since 1972 she's a committed vegan who enjoys spending her time with family and her rescue dogs, cats, pigs, horses, donkeys, alpacas, goats, and sheep.

For more information visit www.JoanneCacciatore.com and www.SelahCarefarm.com.

Thank you for reading

GRIEVING IS LOVING

Here are 5 ways to stay connected with Dr. Jo and support this book:

1.

Take Dr. Jo's online course, Bearing the Unbearable, based on her bestselling book. Visit **wisdomexperience.org** to learn more.

2.

Follow Dr. Jo on Twitter **@dr_cacciatore** to learn about her new work and announcements.

3.

Visit **selahcarefarm.com** to learn about and support Selah Carefarm, the first in the world for those enduring traumatic grief.

4.

Take a photo of your copy of this book and post it on social media, with a few lines explaining how it helped you, or a favorite quote from the book.

5.

Write a review on Amazon. This is very helpful to support the book in reaching more people. Thank you!

WHAT TO READ NEXT
FROM WISDOM PUBLICATIONS

Bearing the Unbearable
Love, Loss, and the Heartbreaking Path of Grief
Joanne Cacciatore

"Simultaneously heartwrenching and uplifting. Cacciatore offers practical guidance on coping with profound and life-changing grief. This book is destined to be a classic . . . [it] is simply the best book I have ever read on the process of grief." —Ira Israel, *The Huffington Post*

The Grace in Living
Recognize It, Trust It, Abide in It
Kathleen Dowling Singh

"Kathleen Dowling Singh has become one of the premier spiritual teachers of grace. . . . Now, she has created *The Grace in Living*, a rich resource encouraging us 'to recognize grace, to trust it, and to embrace grace as our own true nature in every moment of our lives.' We are quite impressed." —*Spirituality and Practice*

The Grace in Aging
Awaken as You Grow Older
Kathleen Dowling Singh

"Don't grow old without it." —Rachel Naomi Remen, MD, author of *Kitchen Table Wisdom*

How to Live Well with Chronic Pain and Illness
A Mindful Guide
Toni Bernhard

"Toni shows us the difference between pain and suffering, and shows us what it can mean for how we live: that our lives can still be joyful."
—David R. Loy, author of *A New Buddhist Path*

Awake at the Bedside
Contemplative Teachings on Palliative and End-of-Life Care
Edited by Koshin Paley Ellison and Matty Weingast

"The greatest degree of inner tranquility comes from the development of love and compassion. The more we care for the happiness of others, the greater is our own sense of well-being. Cultivating a close, warmhearted feeling for others automatically puts the mind at ease. It is the ultimate source of success in life. *Awake at the Bedside* supports this development of love and compassion."
—His Holiness the Dalai Lama

About Wisdom Publications

Wisdom Publications is the leading publisher of classic and contemporary Buddhist books and practical works on mindfulness. To learn more about us or to explore our other books, please visit our website at wisdomexperience.org or contact us at the address below.

Wisdom Publications
199 Elm Street
Somerville, MA 02144 USA

We are a 501(c)(3) organization, and donations in support of our mission are tax deductible.

Wisdom Publications is affiliated with the Foundation for the Preservation of the Mahayana Tradition (FPMT).